# Oh Shenandoah

6

# Simple gifts

Joseph Brackett (1797–1882)
arr. Alexander L'Estrange

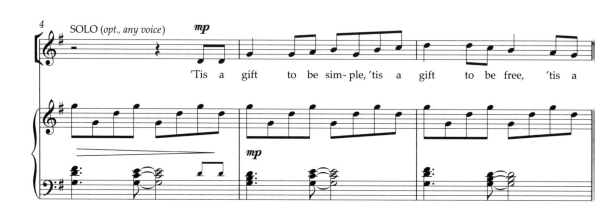

'Tis a gift to be sim- ple, 'tis a gift to be free, 'tis a

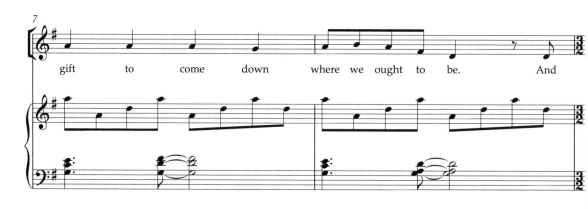

gift to come down where we ought to be. And

when we find our- selves in the place just right, 'twill

be in the val - ley of love and de - light.

When true sim - pli - ci - ty is gained, to

When true sim - pli - ci - ty is gained, to

When true sim - pli - ci - ty is gained, to

bow and to bend we shan't be a - shamed. To turn, turn, will

bow and to bend we shan't be a - shamed. To turn, to turn,

bow and to bend we shan't be a - shamed. To turn, to turn,

be our de-light, till by turn-ing, turn-ing we come_____ round

is our de-light, till by turn-ing, turn-ing we come_____ round

is our de-light, till by turn-ing, turn-ing we come_____ round

right.                                                                        And

when we find our-selves in the place just right,                    'twill

D. S. 𝄋 (p. 10) **to** ⊕ (p. 11) **then to Coda** ⊕ **CODA**

Dedicated to Ward Swingle

# Low-down on the Hoe-down

(Medley: The Arkansas Traveler; Polly Wolly Doodle; Li'l Liza Jane;
Hop up my ladies (three in a row); Old Dan Tucker; Buffalo girls)

Traditional
arr. Alexander L'Estrange

This music is copyright. Photocopying is **ILLEGAL** and is **THEFT**.

14

Hop up my la-dies, three in a row, don't mind the wea-ther when the wind don't blow!

A. SOLO (opt.)
*mf (mock dramatic!)*

Ol' Dan Tuck-er's a migh-ty fine man, washed his face in a fry-ing pan!

Combed his hair with a wa-gon wheel, and died with a tooth-ache in his heel!

20

come out to-night and dance by the light of the moon. The

A.
trav - el - ler re - plied, 'That's all quite true,

but this, I think, is the

S.
get bu - sy on a day that's fair and bright, an'

A.
thing for you to do:

S. ALL
go and patch your roof - ing till it's real - ly good and tight.' But the

# choral basics

*consultant editor* Alexander L'Estrange

**Oh Shenandoah:** this volume is a toe-in-the water introduction to some of the great and much loved American folksongs. Two individual songs are presented here, 'Oh Shenandoah' and 'Simple gifts', along with 'Low-down on the Hoe-down' – a rip-roaring medley of light-hearted line dance tunes.

• • • • • • •

choral basics has been carefully designed to provide rewarding, varied repertoire for beginner choirs. Perfect for singers of all ages, the series offers:

- simple choral arrangements for 2 parts (soprano and alto) and 3 parts (soprano, alto and a combined male-voice part)

- an array of repertoire including world music, spirituals, pop classics, show hits and original pieces

- attractive, idiomatic arrangements, with breathing and vocal range considered for the level

- straightforward piano accompaniments, supporting the vocal lines

- great value for money, with each volume comprising a set of contrasted songs for easy programming

 So build up your confidence and kick-start your choral singing with choral basics !

ISBN10:   0-571-52935-6
EAN13:  978-0-571-52935-3

**FABER $f\!f$ MUSIC**

fabermusic.com

9 780571 529353 >